SOCCER

The Rules
of the Game

Los Angeles

Copyright © 1990 by RGA Publishing Group, Inc.
Published in the United States of America by Price Stern Sloan, Inc.
360 North La Cienega Boulevard, Los Angeles, California 90048

ISBN: 0-8431-2431-8

10 9 8 7 6 5 4 3

The Rules of the Game

In soccer, most of the rules are the same for both professional and youth teams. However, in those cases where the rules are different, youth soccer rules are given at the end of each section.

The Playing Field

THE SOCCER FIELD: All soccer fields are rectangular, but they can vary in size. The field is 100 to 130 yards long and 50 to 100 yards wide. The longer boundary is the **touch line,** and the shorter boundary is the **end line** (or **goal line**). These lines are usually marked with chalk or lime.

A **halfway line** divides the field into 2 squares. The **center circle** has a radius of 10 yards. The point at the circle's center—also the center of the field—is called the **center spot.**

The **coaching areas** are 20 yards long and are 5 yards away from the playing field, parallel to the touch lines on both sides of the field. The coaches may stay in these areas during the game.

In each corner there is a quarter circle with a 1-yard radius, called the **corner area.** A **corner flag,** 2 feet long and 1 foot wide, is attached to a 5-foot-high pole in each corner.

THE GOAL AREA AND THE GOALS: The **goal area** is 6 yards in front of the goal and is 20 yards wide. The **penalty area** extends 18 yards from the goal area, which it encloses, and is 44 yards wide. The **penalty spot,** a line 2 yards long, is 12 yards from the goal line, in the center of the penalty area. The **penalty arc,** with a radius of 10 yards, is a half arc pointing toward midfield. The penalty spot is the midpoint of its radius.

The goals are centered on the goal line and are 8 yards wide and 8 feet tall. The **goal posts** and **crossbar** are usually made of wood, 4" x 4" thick. Goal posts must be white. Nets are made of vinyl or rope mesh. The net slopes out from the back of the goal at a 45 degree angle, so it is always clear whether or not the ball crossed the goal line.

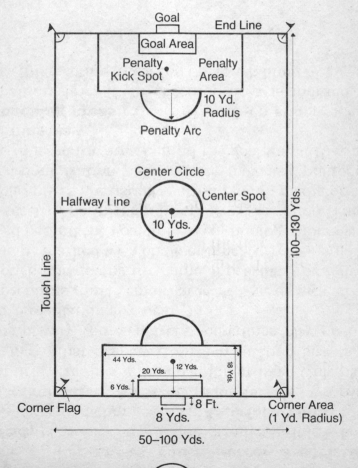

The Playing Field (Youth Only)

The **United States Youth Soccer Association (USYSA)** plays on a regulation size field, unless both teams agree to a change. Each **American Youth Soccer Organization (AYSO)** Division has its own rules about field size, including goal dimensions. Only play-off games must be played on a regulation size field. Teams of very young players sometimes play on one half of a regulation size field.

Spectators must remain at least 3 yards away from the touch line during the game. If possible, these lines should be marked with chalk or lime. No one should be allowed behind the goal line except photographers who have received permission from the organization. These photographers are usually with the news media or the soccer organization. The referee may ask photographers to leave the area behind the goal line if they are disturbing play.

Coaching areas extend 10 yards on either side of the halfway line. Each coaching area is marked by 2 lines intersecting (meeting) the touch line.

Equipment

PLAYERS' UNIFORMS: There is very little equipment used in soccer. The players' uniforms consist of a jersey, shorts, shoes and socks. Most jerseys have numbers on them to help identify the players. The home team wears light-colored jerseys and the visiting team wears dark colors.

Uniform

The goalie's jersey must be a different color than his teammates' to distinguish him or her from other players. The jersey can't be black, however, as this color is worn by the referee and linesmen. A goalie can wear gloves on cold or wet days to keep his or her hands warm and to prevent the ball from slipping. A goalie's jersey may have elbow padding and the shorts may have hip padding.

Soccer shoes are usually made of leather and have molded soles. These shoes may have cleats or studs as long as they do not exceed one half inch in diameter or length. The cleats or studs help keep players from slipping. Studs are usually made of rubber, nylon or a light metal. Different materials are better for different playing conditions. Many studs are removable. Leather or rubber bars may be fitted across the sole instead of studs. They must be at least one half inch wide.

Shin guards are optional, but some players like to wear them under their socks for protection.

Shoes

Shin Guards

THE SOCCER BALL: The soccer ball is round, with a circumference between 27 and 28 inches. The outer layer is usually leather, though vinyl or rubber is sometimes used. The ball should weigh between 14 and 16 ounces. These measurements are for a size 5 ball. Some balls have 32 black-and-white 5-sided panels which help players see the speed, spin and direction of the ball. Other balls are white and have 18 rectangular panels. A soccer ball can withstand about 2 seasons of heavy play.

Soccer Ball

Equipment (Youth Only)

PLAYERS' UNIFORMS: AYSO players have a number on the back of their jerseys. Some teams' jerseys also have numbers on the front. These numbers can't be more than 4 inches high. A 3- or 4-inch AYSO emblem is on the left front of each jersey. Another emblem may be worn on the right sleeve or the front of the shorts.

Either sneakers or soccer shoes may be worn. Rubber cleats are permitted if they are less than one half inch long or wide. AYSO members are required to wear shin guards during games. The organization also encourages players to wear shin guards during practices. No one can play while wearing a cast or splint.

THE SOCCER BALL: The AYSO and USYSA have different weight and circumference requirements.

AYSO BALL

	WEIGHT (OUNCES)	CIRCUMFERENCE (INCHES)
Division 1	14–16	26.5–28.0
Division 2	14–16	26.5–28.0
Division 3	14–16	26.5–28.0
Division 4	12–14	25.0–26.5
Division 5	12–14	25.0–26.5
Division 6	10–12	23.0–25.0
Division K	10–12	23.0–25.0

USYSA BALL

	WEIGHT (OUNCES)	CIRCUMFERENCE (INCHES)
Under 19	14–16	27.0–28.0
Under 16	14–16	27.0–28.0
Under 14	14–16	27.0–28.0
Under 12	11–13	25.0–26.0
Under 10	11–13	25.0–26.0
Under 8	11–12	23.0–24.0
Age 6	11–12	23.0–24.0

For more information on AYSO's divisions and USYSA's age groups, see page 16.

The Players

Each team has 11 players on the field: 5 forwards, 3 halfbacks, 2 fullbacks and 1 goalie.

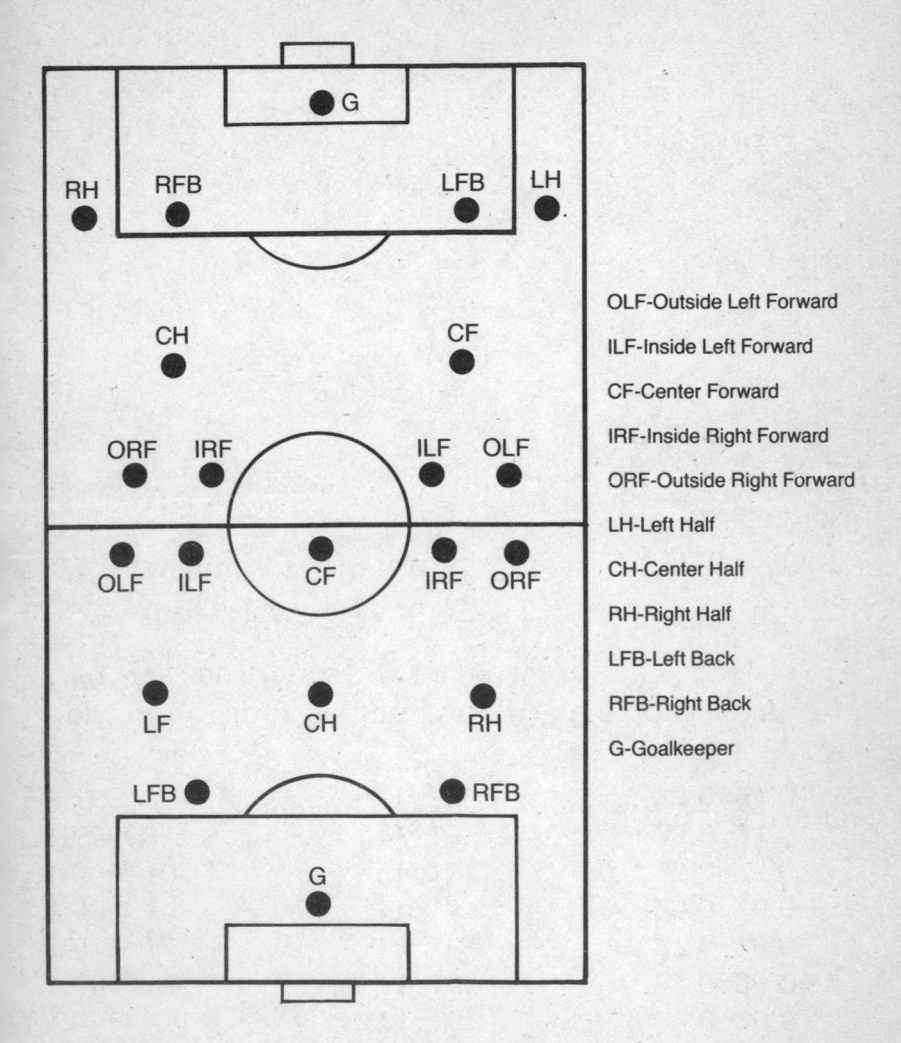

OLF-Outside Left Forward

ILF-Inside Left Forward

CF-Center Forward

IRF-Inside Right Forward

ORF-Outside Right Forward

LH-Left Half

CH-Center Half

RH-Right Half

LFB-Left Back

RFB-Right Back

G-Goalkeeper

HALFBACKS, FULLBACKS AND FORWARDS: The **forwards** are usually the scorers. They need great speed because they cover more of the field than the other players. Forwards must be good dribblers and pass receivers.

Halfbacks are the links for both offense and defense. They must have good all-around skills and the ability to switch roles at a moment's notice. Halfbacks must have a good sense of the game as they often set up plays.

Fullbacks are mostly defensive, so they need to be good at volley kicking and heading. They need to get rid of the ball as quickly as possible to avoid getting tackled. Fullbacks need to prevent shots from being taken, but must not block the goalie's view. If a fullback can force an opponent to the side of the field, it creates a smaller angle from which a shot can be taken.

Head Hit

A **volley kick** sends the ball a long distance. This kick is often used by fullbacks to get the ball into the opponent's side of the field.

THE GOALKEEPER: The **goalkeeper** or **"goalie"** is the only player who can touch, hold or bounce the ball, but the goalie's hand use is limited to the penalty area. If the goalie touches a ball outside the penalty area, the other team is awarded a direct kick.

Classic Catch

The goalie's main job is to prevent the other team from scoring. The goalie is also responsible for calling plays at his or her end of the field, as he or she has the best view of the action. A goalie often tells fullbacks which opponent to cover, yells to his teammates to move away when he can make a save, and appoints a teammate to cover the goal in his or her place if the goalie needs to advance. This "replacement" goalie can't touch the ball with his or her hands or arms. A goalie and a teammate can officially change positions during a break in play after getting the referee's approval.

Soccer is a great sport because it's not just the biggest or strongest people who become great players. Often the smaller players have excellent speed and stamina, which are very important. The only position that "requires" a particular body type is that of the goalkeeper. The goalie should be tall, as increased height gives increased goal coverage. The goalie is often the tallest person on a team.

Soccer is a defensive sport. The attacking team usually has only 7 members on the opponent's side of the field, against 11 defenders. Because of this, the best players are those who develop their own skills while learning to play as a member of a team. These players are willing to give up the ball to a teammate who is in a better position to advance or score the ball. They also try to fake opponents out of position to help their team create scoring opportunities.

The Players (Youth Only)

AYSO and USYSA teams are divided into groups based on age. AYSO refers to its groups as "divisions." AYSO and USYSA age groups are as follows:

AYSO AND USYSA

Division 1	Under 19
Division 2	Under 16
Division 3	Under 14
Division 4	Under 12
Division 5	Under 10

USYSA also has an under 6 group. AYSO Division K is for 5 year olds. AYSO players are put in divisions based on their age on December 31 of the current season. USYSA's players' ages are determined on January 1 of the season.

- USYSA teams are made up of 7 to 18 players.

- AYSO Division 1 and 2 teams must carry between 12 and 18 registered players.

- Teams in Divisions 3 and 6 must have 12 to 15 registered players.

- Division 6 teams can play with up to 9 members on a side instead of 7. Teams that follow this rule may only carry 10 to 13 registered players.

- In order to play, AYSO teams must have 7 people able to start each game.

The Game

OBJECT OF THE GAME: The object is to score the most points by putting the ball into the other team's goal without using the arms or hands. One point is scored per goal.

Kicking Into Other Team's Goal

THE SOCCER SEASON: The professional outdoor soccer season runs from April to August.

HOW LONG IS A GAME?: A professional game consists of two 45-minute periods. Teams switch sides of the field after each period. Half time lasts 5 minutes, unless otherwise agreed upon, during which time players rest and go over game strategy. If a period must be extended for a penalty play because a foul was committed as time ran out, extra time is given only for the actual penalty kick attempt. A scoring play off a rebound in overtime doesn't count.

REFEREES AND LINESMEN: There is 1 **referee** for each game, and his or her ruling is final. Referees usually wear black or black-and-white-striped shirts and black shorts, socks and shoes. The referee has a whistle to signal decisions. Only a team captain is allowed to discuss rule interpretations with the referee.

The referee is also the official timekeeper, keeping track of the playing time per period, including time-outs. He or she usually wears 2 watches.

A player who engages in disorderly conduct may be warned by the referee, who has the option of disqualifying the player. A disqualified player can't be replaced by a teammate.

There are usually 2 **linesmen,** 1 for each half of the field. They indicate a player offside or a ball out of bounds by holding up a flag. They also help the referee award goal kicks, corner kicks and throw-ins. The linesmen indicate what they think happened during a play, but the referee makes the final decision.

Referee   Linesman

SUBSTITUTES: In professional soccer, teams can have only 2 substitutions per game. Once a player leaves the game, he or she cannot return to that game. Originally, no substitutions were allowed, even if a player was injured. The team had to play with fewer players. Since 1967, however, 5 possible substitutes can be named before the game, and 2 can be used if necessary. If a list of up to 5 substitutes is not given to the referee before the game, that team may not substitute during that match.

Substitutions can be made when play stops. If a player leaves the field during play without first telling the referee (for example, to replace a broken shoelace), the opponents are awarded an indirect free kick.

No substitution can be made for a disqualified player.

HOW A GAME STARTS: Each game starts with a **kickoff.** The team that wins the coin toss can either choose to kick off, or choose which goal they would like to defend. The team captain and coach consider factors such as wind conditions and sun glare, keeping in mind that these factors may change (for better or worse) before the next kickoff.

A kickoff also takes place at the beginning of each period and each time a goal is scored. After a goal is scored, the team that gave up the point controls the kickoff. At the start of the second half, the team that did not open the game controls the kickoff.

> For the **kickoff,** a forward kicks the ball from the center spot into the opponent's half of the field. All players must remain in their own halves until the ball has moved at least 27 inches. The opposing players must remain at least 10 yards away from the ball until it is kicked.

On kickoffs, throw-ins, corner kicks and goal kicks, the ball must be touched by another player before the kicker (or thrower) can make a second play. The other team gets an indirect free kick when a player breaks this rule.

The ball remains in play until:

- the game is stopped by the referee.
- time runs out.
- the ball goes out of bounds by crossing the touch line or end line (goal line), regardless of whether it is a ground or air ball. If the ball hits a goal post, crossbar, corner flag or an official, and rebounds back onto the field, it is still in play. Continuous play is one reason why soccer is so appealing to fans and players.

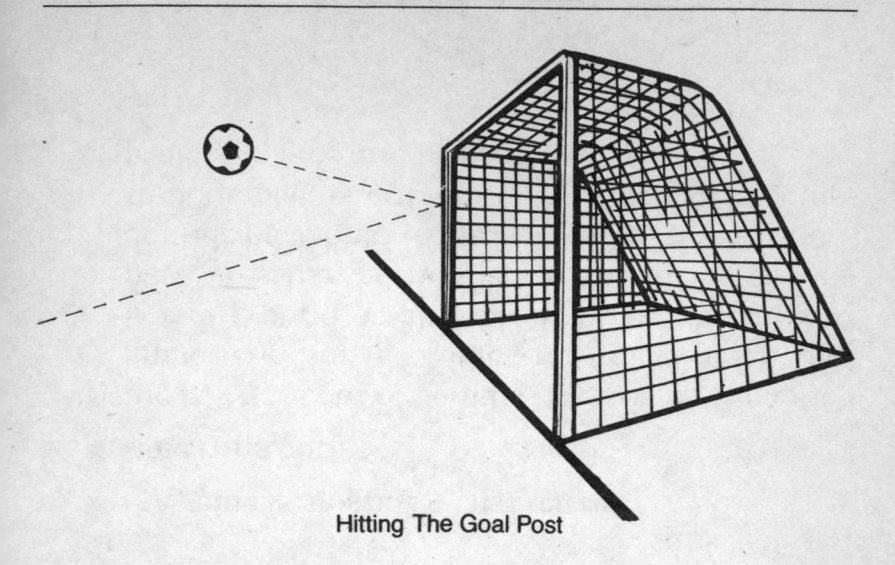

Hitting The Goal Post

DROP BALL: If the referee calls for a time out—for example, when a player is injured—the game resumes with a **drop ball** where the ball was last in play. If the game stops while the ball is in the penalty area, the drop ball is performed in the nearest spot outside the penalty area.

1. The referee drops the ball from waist height between 1 player from each team.

2. The ball is in play once it hits the ground.

Drop Ball

THROW-IN: If the ball goes out of bounds over a touch line, the team that last touched the ball loses possession. A member of the opposing team returns the ball to play with a **throw-in.**

1. The player stands at the point where the ball crossed the line and throws the ball overhead using both hands.

2. The player's feet must remain on the ground during the actual throw, although he or she may run up to the touch line before releasing the ball.

3. If the player throws the ball incorrectly, a member of the opposite team gets a chance at a throw-in.

Throw-In

GOAL KICK: When an offensive player accidentally kicks the ball across the end line, the referee stops play. Play restarts with a defensive **goal kick** from the penalty area.

1. The referee puts the ball on the ground in the half of the goal area where the ball went out of bounds.

2. A defending player kicks the ball upfield.

3. The offensive team must remain out of the penalty area until the ball is kicked.

4. If the ball does not clear the penalty area, the defending player gets another chance to kick the ball. The ball is returned to the same spot as the first goal kick.

Goal Kick

CORNER KICK: If a defensive player causes the ball to cross the end line, the opponents are awarded a **corner kick.**

1. The referee places the ball in the corner area closest to where the ball left the field.

2. Defensive players must remain 10 yards away from the ball until it is kicked.

3. The kicker usually lofts the ball to a teammate who tries to head it in for a point.

4. If the goalie is positioned well before the kick, he or she can often catch the ball before an opponent can try to head the ball into the goal.

INDIRECT FREE KICK: A dangerous play, sideline coaching and a player offside are all examples of broken rules. When someone breaks a rule, the referee awards the opposing team with an **indirect free kick.**

1. This kick takes place where the ball was in play when the rule was broken.

2. The ball must be kicked once before a scoring attempt can be made.

3. When a team is awarded an indirect free kick less than 10 yards from the opponent's goal, the opposing players can stand on the goal line between goal posts during the kick.

4. If the ball accidentally moves off a defender's foot into the goal, the goal is not counted and the referee awards the opponents a corner kick.

DIRECT FREE KICK: A **direct free kick** is awarded when a player commits a major foul.

1. The direct free kick is taken from the spot where the penalty occurred.

2. Opposing players must be 10 yards away from the ball.

3. If the foul was committed by an offensive player in the opponent's penalty area, his or her team must remain outside the penalty area during the kick.

4. The ball must be kicked upfield—a player can't pass the ball to the goalie for a clearing kick.

5. The ball is not in play until it has cleared the area.

A **clearing kick** carries the ball from one end of the field to the other.

The 9 Major Fouls

1. Charging from behind
2. Handling the ball
3. Holding or jumping at an opponent
4. Kicking an opponent
5. Kicking the ball while it's held by the goalie
6. Pushing
7. Striking
8. Tripping
9. Violent charging

Tripping

Jumping

Handling

Pushing

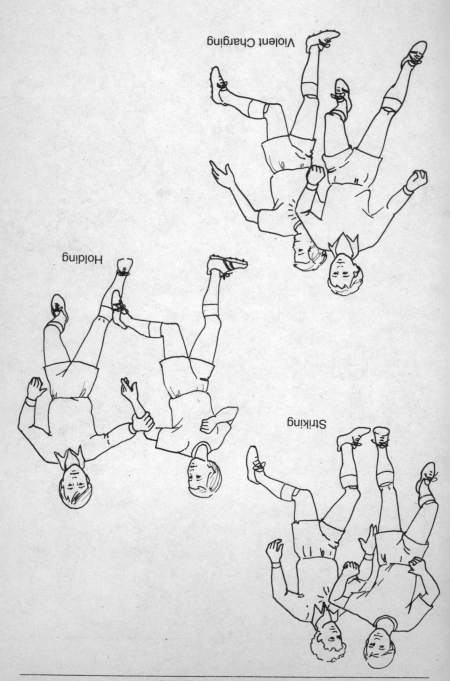

Violent Charging

Holding

Striking

Charging From Behind

Kicking

PENALTY KICK: When the foul is committed by a defender in his own penalty area, the other team gets a **penalty kick** from the penalty spot. Only the goalie remains to protect against scoring. His or her feet must not move until the ball is kicked, but if a goal is scored, the referee makes no call against a goalie who breaks this rule. If the goal doesn't score but the goalie breaks this rule, the kick is retaken.

Everyone but the goalie and the kicker must be outside the penalty area and at least 10 yards away from the ball. If a defensive player breaks this rule, the kick is replayed. If an offensive player breaks this rule, any resulting score from the first kick is not counted and the kick is replayed. If the kicker kicks the ball twice before another player touches it, the other team is awarded an indirect free kick.

Of course, catching a goal attempt is better than deflecting the ball, because the opponents will not get a second chance to score. Sometimes, however, it is impossible to catch a shot. If the ball is very high, the goalie may punch the ball over the crossbar.

Punching Over

If the goalie catches the ball, he or she can take 3 steps before kicking the ball back into play, or 4 steps (between bouncing the ball) before throwing it. A goalie can use a one-handed throw. If the goalie takes more than the number of steps allowed, the other team is awarded an indirect free kick. If an unguarded teammate is nearby, the goalie can roll the ball to that player. Most of the time, throwing the ball to a teammate is better than kicking, because throws are usually more accurate. But the goalie has to make his or her decision based on each situation.

One-Handed Throw

Roll

OFFSIDE: The most complicated rule in soccer is the **offside** call.

- If the ball is between a player and the opponent's goal, he or she is never offside.

- If the ball is not between the offensive player and the goal, there must be at least 2 defenders between this offensive player and the goal, or the player is offside.

An offside charge is called while the ball is being passed, not after a player receives the ball. Therefore, once a player receives the ball he or she can advance without worrying about this call. A player is never offside during goal kicks, drop balls, corner kicks, or when the ball is last played or touched by an opponent.

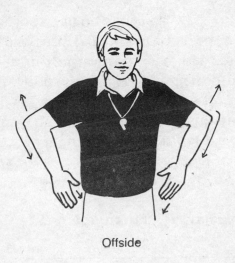

Offside

The Game (Youth Only)

LENGTH OF GAME: The length of each game period for AYSO and USYSA is as follows:

AYSO PERIOD LENGTHS

Division 1	40 minutes
Division 2	35 minutes
Division 3	30 minutes
Division 4	25 minutes
Division 5	25 minutes
Division 6	20 minutes

USYSA GAME LENGTHS

Under 19	45 minutes
Under 16	40 minutes
Under 14	35 minutes
Under 12	30 minutes
Under 10	decided by coaches
Under 8	decided by coaches
Age 6	decided by coaches

REFEREES: There are usually 2 referees in youth games.

SUBSTITUTES:

AYSO: AYSO team members must play at least half of each game. The referee will allow substitutions once in the middle of each period during a normal break in play. Substitutions will also be allowed at half time. There is no limit to the number of players who can be changed. If overtime periods are played to break a tie, free substitutions will be allowed.

Free substitutions mean that the coach can change players as often as he or she wants. There is also no limit to the number of players who are changed. These substitutions are usually done when a team changes its defensive/offensive role.

When a player is substituted because of injury, he or she may not return to the game until the next quarter. However, if the team plays without 1 player rather than sending in a substitute, the injured player may return to the game in the same quarter.

Players who arrive late to a game may not be allowed to play the regular time limit. Players arriving during the first quarter play half a game. Players arriving after the first quarter are only guaranteed 1 quarter of play.

USYSA: When play is stopped for a throw-in, players from the team in possession of the ball are allowed to enter or leave the game. When play is stopped before a goal kick, after a goal is scored or when a player is injured, both teams are allowed to substitute players. Substitutions are also permitted at half time. Teams can make as many substitutions as they like.

Definitions of Soccer Terms

Advancing from the goal: A move used by the goalie when he or she leaves the immediate goal area to challenge an offensive player who broke past the defense. This tactic reduces scoring chances because there are fewer angles to shoot from.

Advantage: The offensive team has an advantage when a defensive player commits a foul, but can't gain control of the ball. Play continues. A foul isn't called because the offensive team keeps possession of the ball.

Angle of possibility: The angle measured from the ball to each goal post. The larger the angle, the greater the chance of making the shot.

Banana shot: A spinning shot that dips in the air and is difficult for goalies to stop.

Blanket defense: Tight coverage of the goal, with more defensive than offensive players.

Breakaway: When a player possessing the ball has cleared the defenders and bears down on the goalie.

Carrying: When the goalkeeper takes more than 4 steps while possessing the ball. This is a minor offense, awarding the opposing team an indirect free kick.

Center pass: A pass which moves the ball from the side of the field to center field.

Change of pace: When a dribbler gets as close as possible to a defender before speeding past him or her.

Charging: A legal charge is used by a defender to gain control of the ball. The defender nudges the opponent's shoulder while both players are running, hoping the opponent will lose control of the ball. Both players must have at least one foot on the ground during the moment of contact.

Clearing kick: A kick that carries the ball from one end of the field to the other.

Corner kick: See "The Game" section.

Creating space: A player creates space by moving into an open area. Creating space makes it easier to move the ball between teammates because there are no opponents in the area.

Cross: A kick from one side of the field to the other.

Decisive space: The part of the field in front of and around the goal.

Decoy play: A play designed to move the opponents out of position, making it easier to score.

Defensive containment: Holding back an opponent while trying to get the ball.

Direct free kick: See "The Game" section.

Double pass: When a passer receives the ball back from the receiver.

Double foul: When opposing players commit fouls at the same time. In this case, a drop ball resumes play.

Dribbling: Moving the ball by short, controlled kicks.

Drop ball: See "The Game" section.

English: An aerial spin a skilled player can give a ball. If a player can control the English, he or she can move the ball around obstacles, such as the goalie.

Feeder: A player who gives the ball to a high scorer.

First time kick: Kicking the ball before it bounces.

Flat front: A move in which attackers or defenders cross the field in a straight line, forming a barrier.

Flick pass: A deceptive side pass done off the ankle, usually made while dribbling.

Foul: A foul is a play which breaks the rules. When a minor foul is committed, the opposing team is awarded an indirect free kick. A major foul gives the opponents a penalty kick.

Freezing the ball: Keeping the ball without advancing it to the opponent's side of the field. This stalling technique prevents the opponents from getting the ball and scoring.

Fundamentals: The basic techniques—dribbling, heading, kicking, passing, tackling and trapping.

Goal kick: See "The Game" section.

Goal mouth: The area directly in front of the goal.

Half volley kick: A kick made just after the ball bounces off the ground, resulting in a hard low drive.

Handling: Use of the arms or hands to direct the ball or protect oneself. Handling is a major foul. Exception: Girls may cross their arms in front of their chests for protection when they trap a ball.

Hat trick: Three goals scored by a player in the same match.

Heading: Using the flat, center portion of the forehead to pass or shoot.

Heeling: Using the heel to pass or kick the ball.

Hooking: Deflecting a ball from an opponent to a teammate by using an outstretched leg.

Indirect free kick: See "The Game" section.

Instep: The top of your foot where the shoelaces lie. Part of the foot most often in contact with the ball.

Inswinger ball: A corner kick which curves toward the goal.

Jockeying: A method of covering an opponent who is in possession of the ball. A player jockeys by pretending to move in a certain direction or pretending to kick the ball, hoping to confuse the opponent.

Jump kick: Kicking the ball by swinging either foot at the ball after jumping into the air.

Kick to a spot: Kicking the ball to an open area where a teammate can reach it before an opponent.

Leading pass: A pass made ahead of a running teammate, but in his or her path, so that the ball can be reached without breaking stride.

Linkmen: Another term for halfbacks.

Lob: A high kick without much power, usually to send the ball over the defense.

Mark: Guarding a player very closely.

Negative passing: Passing down the field, rather than toward the opponent's end.

Net-minder: Another term for the goalie.

Obstruction: Using the body to block an opponent from the ball, resulting in an indirect free kick.

One-touch: Trapping and passing the ball in 1 motion.

Outswinger ball: One that swings away from the goal off a corner kick. The goalie often advances, leaving the goal open to scoring plays.

Overhead volley: A kick made while the top half of the body is falling down and a leg snaps at the ball in midair. The second leg leaves the ground as the kicking leg snaps. The palms should be facing the ground to cushion the fall.

Pigeon holes: The 2 upper corners of the goal, which are hard to defend.

Pitch: British term for a soccer field.

Place kick: A kick delivered to a motionless ball.

Pressure defense: A defense which forces the offense to make a mistake and lose possession of the ball.

Pulling the book: When a player is guilty of misconduct, the referee writes his or her name in a black book. If the player's name appears 3 times, he or she is disqualified.

Punching: A term for the way a goalie blocks a high shot by deflecting it over the crossbar.

Retreating funnel defense: A defensive move in which the goalie and fullbacks retreat toward their goal. The other defenders stall the attack and make it hard for the offense to break through.

Ride the ball: When trapping, cushioning the body by "giving" under impact. This enables the ball to fall directly in front of the player, rather than bouncing off in another direction.

Save: Credited to a defender who blocks a scoring attempt.

Screening: Trying to move the opponent out of position by temporarily placing oneself between the player and the ball.

Second touch shot: Deflecting a ball off a penalty kick so that an immediate shot on goal can be taken by a teammate. This technique often fools goalies because they expect the first player to try to score.

Shepherding: Giving ground to an offensive player in possession of the ball to get him or her to move in a particular direction.

Six-yarder: A goal kick.

Sliding tackle: Sliding into the ball with an extended leg to get the ball away from an opponent. If you trip the other player, but touch the ball first, there is no penalty.

Spearhead formation: The 3 middle forwards approach the goal area while the 2 outer forwards try to move the defensive fullbacks out of position so the middle forwards can score.

Square pass: A direct pass across the field to an advancing player.

Stopper: A defender in the front center of the penalty area, usually a halfback.

Strikers: The forwards.

Support: Playing near the ball to increase the chance of controlling it.

Swiss bolt: Soccer game played with 5 attackers, 5 defenders and a reserve defender (the "bolt").

Switch: When a teammate covers a position for another player.

Target player: A player near the goal to whom other players try to give the ball.

Through-pass: A pass shot between (through) defenders. The ball usually travels behind at least 1 opponent.

Throw-in: See "The Game" section.

Torpedo header: A move in which the player dives at the ball for a head shot, resembling a torpedo.

Trapping: Method of cushioning the ball against part of the body (chest, thigh, foot, etc.) so that it falls in front of the player and is easily controlled when it hits the ground.

Turnover: Term used to describe the change of teams in possession of the ball.

Two-touch: Controlling the ball in the first touch, and passing/shooting on the second.

Volleying: Kicking a midair ball (without trapping or stopping).

Volley kick: A kick that sends the ball a long distance. A volley kick is often used by fullbacks to get the ball into the opponent's side of the field.

Wall pass: A pass used when there are 2 offensive players and 1 defender. The player with the ball passes to a teammate, runs past the defender, and receives the ball back.

Wing: An outside forward.

Yellow card: Players who repeatedly display unsportsman-like conduct receive a yellow card from the referee, warning them that they may be ejected.

Zone defense: Defending a certain portion of the field rather than guarding a particular player.